Mathematics from

This Mathematics from Design Activity Book is based on the Shape, Space and Measures unit of television programmes in the TVM series which was produced for Channel 4 Schools by Like Minds Limited.

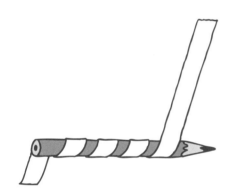  

Introduction

The activity pages in this book are designed to be used with 7–11 year-olds. In particular, they are intended to support the unit Shape, Space and Measures in the Channel 4 Schools maths series TVM.

The general aim of this book is to increase the enjoyment, understanding and involvement of children in maths, through art and design. It explores the links between these under five broad headings – Printing, Weaving, Tiling, Folding and Reflecting. The maths content focuses on shape, space and measures.

The book is divided into five sections each of which extends the content of the television programmes. It could equally stand alone to complement independent work on the five separate areas as listed previously. There are six activity sheets per section which allow for differentiated use and which can be easily adapted or used with children working individually, in pairs or in groups. As far as possible the activities use equipment/resources which are normally available in schools. Some activity sheets use Resource sheets which are at the back of the book. Two teacher's pages introduce each section and are designed to give an overview of the activities on the pages that follow. They also provide some extension material for each activity.

©1996 Channel Four Learning Ltd

All rights reserved

The activity pages within this publication may be photocopied for use within the purchasing institution only

Written by
Anne Woodman

Edited by
Liz Meenan

Designed by
Andrew Barron &
Collis Clements
Associates

Illustrated by
David Farris
Cedric Knight

Printed by
Colour Quest Ltd

Further information about Channel 4 Schools programmes and accompanying resources is available from

Channel 4 Schools
PO Box 100
Warwick
CV34 6TZ

Contents

Printing
Teacher's notes	4
1 Printing puzzle	6
2 Monoprint	7
3 Carbon-paper printing	8
4 Overlaps	9
5 Four-square patterns	10
6 Alphabet prints	11

Weaving
Teacher's notes	12
1 Paper looms	14
2 Symmetrical paper looms	15
3 Decorated container	16
4 Woven heart basket	17
5 God's Eye weaving	18
6 Repeating patterns	19

Tiling
Teacher's notes	20
1 Does it tessellate?	22
2 New tiles from old	23
3 Cut and slide	24
4 Tiling pattern	25
5 Pentomino tiles	26
6 Cut and rotate	27

Folding
Teacher's notes	28
1 Spring things	30
2 Double star	31
3 Imagining	32
4 Tissue tiles	33
5 Magic grid	34
6 Cut and fold back 1	35

Reflecting
Teacher's notes	36
1 How many ways?	38
2 Cut and fold back 2	39
3 Model symmetry	40
4 Picture gallery	41
5 Find the mirror line	42
6 Paper cut-outs	43

Resource sheets
Squared dotty grid (1cm)	44
Isometric grid (1cm)	45
Squared broken-line grid (1cm)	46
Activity-page record sheet	47
Additional information	48

Mathematics from Design
Resources   Inside back cover

© 1996 Channel Four Learning Ltd **Mathematics from Design**

Printing

Teacher's notes

1
Printing puzzle *page 6*

This activity uses rubber-stamp prints and ink pads which are easily accessible and quick to set up. The stamps might be linked to a theme, e.g. Christmas motifs.

The children have to solve a spatial problem which requires them to plan, work systematically and position prints by following rules.

One possible solution is:

A	B	C	D
B	C	D	A
C	D	A	B
D	A	B	C

☞ Discuss the strategies the children used to solve this problem and correct solutions. How are other solutions the same as/different to that given above?

☞ Extension: Follow the same rules but use:

a five stamps and a 5 x 5 grid;
b six stamps and a 6 x 6 grid.

2
Monoprint *page 7*

In this children create a symmetrical print of lines at right angles to each other. A printing roller and laminated board are required for this activity but one of each is sufficient for a group. Old picture frames (with glass intact) or melamine trays make excellent printing bases.

Before the children peel the print off, ask them, how do you think the print will be the same as (different from) the design in the ink? Language related to lines can be promoted, e.g. who has drawn the lines parallel to the edges of the tray? Are there horizontal or vertical lines? You may also introduce the term 'perpendicular' as an alternative to 'at right angles to'. Discussion might also centre around positive and negative images and the links with photographic negatives and their prints.

☞ One variation using cut paper shapes is suggested on the activity sheet but encourage the children to experiment, to see what will happen if …?

3
Carbon-paper printing *page 8*

Carbon paper, used here, is an excellent, cheap, inspiring but under-used medium for investigating multiple symmetrical images. Carbon images are not traditionally thought of as a form of printing but are exactly that. The thinner the paper used, the better. Ideally, the children should lean on pads of newspaper and press firmly over their line design with a ball-point pen to give the best carbon images.

The children have to design a word pattern with one line of symmetry. Problem-solving arises in the rules required for the design of the letters and the use of space.

☞ Variations and extensions include:

a creating symmetrical carbon patterns with two or three lines of symmetry;
b experimental folding to 'see what happens if …?';
c giving a design constraint, e.g. Design a snowflake pattern.

4
Overlaps *page 9*

Rubber stamps of common geometric plane shapes are needed for this. These are readily available in most schools and provide a simple means of creating printed images.

By encouraging the children to find polygons created in the overlaps of two printed geometric shapes, the activity requires several problem-solving skills, e.g. planning, trial and improve, accuracy, perseverance and visualisation as well as the ability to recognise different polygons.

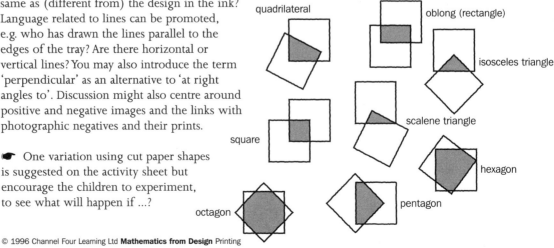

© 1996 Channel Four Learning Ltd **Mathematics from Design** Printing

If two squares are chosen, it is possible to make six of the eight shapes suggested on the activity sheet –

scalene triangle, isosceles triangle, pentagon, hexagon, square and octagon.

💬 Discuss: Why isn't it possible to make the equilateral triangle or the kite?

☞ Extend the activity by asking the children to design a strip pattern or sheet of gift wrap systematically covered with overlapping prints.

5
Four-square patterns *page 10*

Press-Print, sold in 30cm x 30cm sheets, is the preferred material for creating the printing block for this activity. In advance, cut the sheets into 5cm squares. A paper cutter can be used, but cut the squares accurately.

In this activity, the children create a square printing block with specific design features and find different ways of arranging these in a 2 x 2 square and recording their results in coded form.

💬 Afterwards, display some of the codes but not the patterns and ask, what can you tell me about the pattern this code belongs to without seeing it?

☞ Variations include experimenting with printing blocks of other shapes and planning how to arrange these to create patterns with different symmetries or which translate, or combine symmetry and translation.

6
Alphabet prints *page 11*

This activity is a group project in which the children have to design a Press-Print alphabet which will print correctly, i.e. the letters on the Press-Print need to be mirror images of the actual letters.

You can link this with the history of printing. Printing presses had to use reversals of letters and the words scanned from right to left on the printing blocks. Some children may have the printing sets made from rubber letters which fit into slots.

Sorting capital letters in different ways provides a good source of handling data.

For example:

	rotational symmetry	no rotational symmetry
one or more lines of symmetry		
no lines of symmetry		

💬 What other ways can the children think of to classify the letters?
Can they design appropriate sorting diagrams for the classifications and label them correctly?

☞ Extension: If '.' and '?', '+', '-', 'x', '÷' and '=' and numerals are designed in the same way, the children could create short sentences, questions or calculations.

References and resources

Assorted general and geometric rubber-stamp sets (Philip & Tacey)

Basic Shapes Stamps (Taskmaster)

Press-Print and Cromar Paint (Berol Ltd)

The Know How Book of Print and Paint (Usborne)

Tiles – Leapfrog Action Book (Tarquin Publications)

© 1996 Channel Four Learning Ltd **Mathematics from Design** Printing

Printing puzzle

You need

✔ Four rubber stamps (up to 4cm x 4cm), each a different design

✔ ink pad

✔ scrap paper

▶ Place a rubber-stamp print in each square so that there is:

a a different print in each row;
b a different print in each column.

Practise on scrap paper first.

Challenge

What about a different print in each diagonal as well?

2 Monoprint

You need

- ✔ A4 white paper
- ✔ plasticene board or similar laminated surface at least A4 in size
- ✔ black water-based printing ink or sticky paint such as Cromar
- ✔ printing roller
- ✔ pencil

▶ Spread the ink with a roller over the board until the tray is covered with a thin even layer onto which your paper will fit.

▶ Using the sharp end of a pencil, draw a pattern of lines of different lengths at right angles to each other.

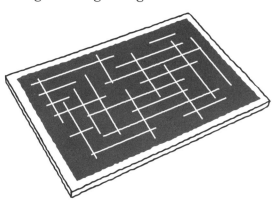

Don't let the ink dry out.

▶ Lay accurately a piece of paper over your design.
Rub the palm of the hand over the surface of the paper.
Try not to let the paper move.

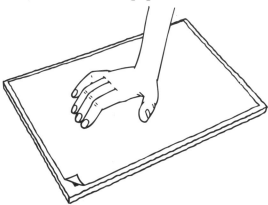

▶ Turn back one corner of your print and peel off the paper carefully.

You have created a **monoprint**.

▶ Find out what 'mono' means.
How is the print the same as the design in the base?
How is it different?

▶ You might also:

– Cut out shapes of one family, e.g. pentagons.

– Prepare the inked tray then place the shapes on it before putting the paper on top to make a print.

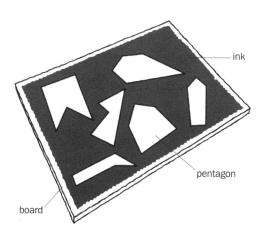

© 1996 Channel Four Learning Ltd **Mathematics from Design** Printing

3

Carbon-paper printing

You need

- ✔ A4 sheet of carbon paper
- ✔ A4 sheet of thin white paper
- ✔ pencil
- ✔ ruler
- ✔ colouring materials
- ✔ ball-point pen
- ✔ newspaper

▶ Fold the sheet of A4 paper in half lengthwise so that the fold is a line of symmetry.

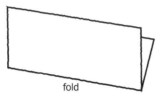

▶ Trim the open edges of the folded sheet to make an interesting shape. Do not cut too much away!

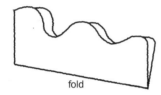

▶ Write in pencil a 5- or 6-letter word in double-lined capital letters. Make the letters as high as possible and touching each other.

▶ Insert a sheet of folded carbon paper, carbon side facing out, pushing it down to meet the fold on the paper.

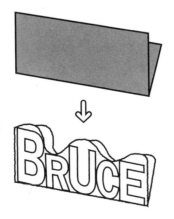

▶ Trace over your letters with a ball-point pen, pressing firmly. (It helps if you lean on a pad of newspaper.)

What do you think will happen?

▶ Open up your design. You have now made a symmetrical transfer print.

▶ Colour symmetrically parts of your design.

Challenge

What would this half-word say if you placed a mirror on the dotted line?

▶ Design a half-word on the fold so that, when you open your carbon transfer print, you see the whole word.

4

Overlaps

You need

✔ rubber stamps of 2-D shapes such as squares, triangles, etc.

✔ ink pad

✔ paper

▶ Choose a rubber stamp of:

either a **square**
or a **rectangle**
or a **triangle**.

▶ Using only the rubber stamp you choose, find out what shapes you can make in the overlap if you print the shape twice.

For example, by overlapping two squares, you can make this right-angled triangle.

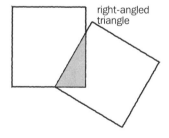

right-angled triangle

▶ Is it possible to make all of the shapes named below in the overlap?

Name the ones possible on your pictures.

- **square**
- **kite**
- **hexagon**
- **pentagon**
- **octagon**
- **scalene triangle**
- **equilateral triangle**
- **isosceles triangle**

▶ Now try using any two of the three stamps, e.g. a square and a triangle.

See what shapes you can make in the overlaps.

© 1996 Channel Four Learning Ltd **Mathematics from Design** Printing

Four-square patterns

You need

- ✔ water-based printing ink
- ✔ scissors
- ✔ A3 white paper
- ✔ sticky tape
- ✔ small piece of card
- ✔ 6cm square of Press-Print
- ✔ pencil
- ✔ roller
- ✔ flat tray

▶ Place the Press-Print square flat on the desk.

Using a pencil, draw a path on the tile from one corner to the opposite corner.

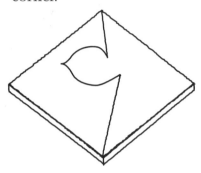

▶ Press in a design on one side. These marks are made with a pencil point.

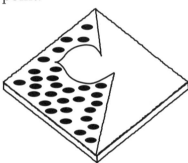

▶ Flip the tile over and number the sides as shown.

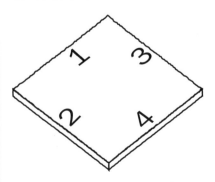

▶ Tape on a handle of card.

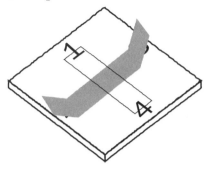

▶ Roll out a thin layer of printing ink on a tray or other flat base until the ink is smooth.

Print the tile four times to make a larger square. Code it as shown.

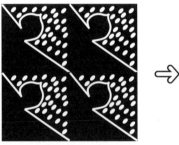 ⇒

1	1
1	1

means **edge 1** was **at the top** of each of the four prints.

▶ Print as many different patterns made in this way as you can. Write the code for each one.

Compare how many patterns you found with a friend.

Is your code the same as your friend's for each pattern?

© 1996 Channel Four Learning Ltd **Mathematics from Design** Printing

Alphabet prints

You need

✔ 1 uncut sheet of Press-Print
✔ scissors
✔ pencil
✔ ruler
✔ roller
✔ printing tray
✔ water-based printing ink
✔ scrap paper

This is a project for a group of four to six children.

▶ Rule gridlines with a felt-tipped pen onto the Press-Print to divide it up into 5cm squares.
Cut the sheet into 5cm squares. Make sure you do this accurately.

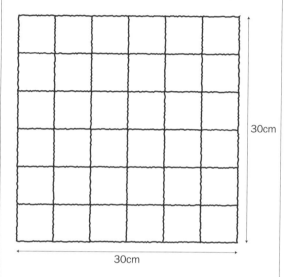

▶ Design a double-lined capital letter on each square so that it will print facing the right way. Each letter should be 5cm in height and about 4cm wide.
Design on rough paper first.

▶ Decide who will design each letter so that the complete alphabet is obtained.

▶ You could imprint patterns onto the letters, e.g. with a pencil point.

Roll out a thin layer of printing ink on a tray or other flat base until the ink is smooth.

▶ Try printing your own name.

© 1996 Channel Four Learning Ltd **Mathematics from Design** Printing

Weaving

Teacher's notes

1
Paper looms *page 14*

Paper looms can introduce children to the basic principles and language of weaving. The advantage of this technique is that is much quicker to achieve results than traditional weaving with yarns. Also paper is readily accessible. Before undertaking this activity, focus children's attention on the range of paper available so that children will be more adventurous in their choice of materials and may bring in interesting examples from home to incorporate in their weavings. On this page, the children experiment with the basic 'one over, one under' weaving using strips of different widths as the weft. They are encouraged to generalise about the shapes in the weaving then challenged to modify what they have done to:

a create a warp and weft which will produce squares only;

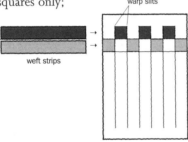

To do this, the children need to realise that the widths of the weft slits and the warp strips need to be equal. This requires careful measuring.

b create a warp and weft on which parallelograms can be produced.

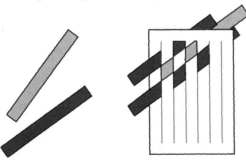

One possible solution is to weave the strips (weft) so that they are slanted.

☛ A further challenge is to design a warp which will generate trapezia only when the weft strips are woven in.

2
Symmetrical paper looms *page 15*

Ideally, children undertaking this activity should have tried **Activity 1 (Paper looms)** but this is not essential. This activity encourages the children to experiment with cutting warps which are not straight lines on a symmetrical paper loom and to investigate the effect when the paper weft is woven in. When the cuts in the warp are made from, for example, zigzag lines, different polygons are created when the weft is added.

You might usefully discuss if the weaving is symmetrical in every aspect. For example, to be totally symmetrical, congruent strips of the same colour need to balance or mirror each other at each side of the weaving. Often such weavings have symmetry of shape but not colour, unless a plan is devised for a totally symmetrical effect.

The children are challenged to design a loom for a non-symmetrical weaving.

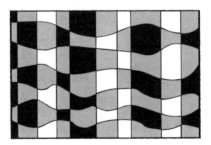

To do this, the weft needs to be designed without folding the paper. This particular example shows the effect of a weft made from curved lines.

In the final challenge children are asked to create a weaving in which two 'diamonds' can be seen.

The wefts on the loom will look similar to this:

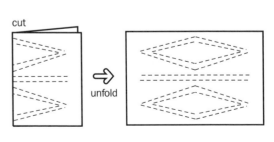

© 1996 Channel Four Learning Ltd **Mathematics from Design** Weaving

3
Decorated container page 16

Ideally, children undertaking this activity should have tried **Activity 1 (Paper looms)** or **Activity 2 (Symmetrical paper looms)**, but this is not essential.

In this activity, the children apply their knowledge of basic 'flat' weaving and adapt it for covering faces of junk containers (or containers they have made from card nets) with weavings designed specifically for this purpose. Careful planning and measurement are essential, particularly if the item is to have a specific purpose, e.g. a container for pencils. If cylinders or junk cuboids are to be used, as suggested, get the children to bring in items they will need in advance. Cardboard containers, similar to the type in which custard powder is stored, are ideal. But cans are also ideal provided removal of the lid has left no sharp edges.

This can has been converted into an attractive container by the addition of a woven cover.

4
Woven heart basket page 17

This woven paper heart is a popular Christmas tree decoration in Denmark where part of the preparation for Christmas is to gather round the table and make decorations for the tree. The baskets are often filled with sweets before being hung on the tree. Enthusiasts have gone on to create very elaborate versions, examples of which can be seen in **References and resources**.

It is best if you make one of these baskets in advance so that you can anticipate potential problems the children might have. Once you have made one, they are comparatively easy to make and very satisfying.

After the final strip is woven in, the weaver may have to adjust the strips slightly to make the completed heart look tidier. If one of the two rectangles mentioned on the activity page is made from gift wrap and the other from plain paper, a very pleasing effect is obtained.

5
God's Eye weaving page 18

This sheet introduces the technique for creating a simple God's Eye weaving. These weavings are commonly seen in parts of Mexico. They symbolise the eye of God, in the belief that the eye of God will protect a child. A God's Eye can be made for each year of a child's life, initially by an adult and then by the children themselves. The age can be represented by the number of colours used. Many patterns can be discussed during their construction, e.g. repetitive patterns of movement, texture and colour. On completion, ask, what can you tell me about the structure of the God's Eye? Encourage the children to see that it has rotational symmetry of order 4.

Afterwards, the children are encouraged to think how to adapt their knowledge and skills to weave on sticks other shapes such as rectangles, kites and hexagons.

6
Repeating patterns page 19

Weaving patterns (drawn or actually made) can be analysed and the relationship between the warp and weft expressed in binary code, e.g. **O** – the weft thread goes **over** the warp, **U** – the weft thread goes **under** the warp. Weavings with repeating elements can be examined and the instructions for each repeat written in this binary code. Children are given opportunities to try writing in this binary code on the activity sheet.

Weaving patterns can be difficult and time-consuming to draw accurately but children who show an interest will benefit from using the program Weaving (from the Video Maths software listed above).

References and resources

Christmas Hearts,
Leif Kragh
(Mathematics Teaching 145)

Mathematics through Art and Design,
Woodman and Albany
(Collins Educational)

The Art Machine Pattern Book
(Tarquin Publications)

Weaving from Disc 1,
Video Maths Computer Software
(GSN Software Ltd)

1 Paper looms

You need

✔ glue
✔ scissors
✔ sheet of A4 paper
✔ strips of paper in assorted colours, 21cm long (the width of A4 paper)

▶ Draw a 2cm frame around your A4 paper.

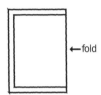

▶ Fold it in half widthwise.

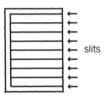

▶ Make slits about 2cm apart at right angles to the fold, ending at the frame.

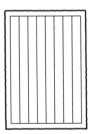

▶ Unfold the loom and place it frame-side down.

▶ Now weave the coloured strips of paper in and out of the vertical slits.

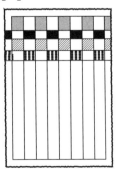

The slits act as the vertical **warp** for your weaving. The strips form the horizontal **weft**.

▶ Experiment with:

– paper of different colours, patterns and textures;

– weaving strips of different widths;

– inventing a rule for the order in which you weave the strips.
For example:

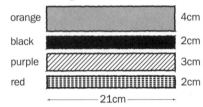

Glue the ends of the strips in position.

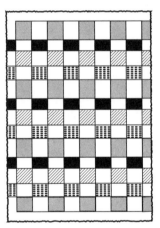

What is the same about all the shapes in your weaving?
What is different?

Using another paper loom made in the same way, make a weaving of squares only.

Or weave your strips so that you end up with parallelograms.

14

© 1996 Channel Four Learning Ltd **Mathematics from Design** Weaving

2

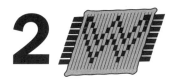

Symmetrical paper looms

You need

- ✔ glue
- ✔ scissors
- ✔ sheets of A4 paper
- ✔ strips of paper in assorted colours, 21cm long (the width of A4 paper)

▶ Make this woven pattern as shown.

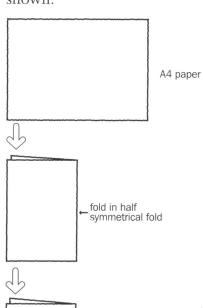

A4 paper

⬇

fold in half
symmetrical fold

⬇

make zigzag cuts

⬇

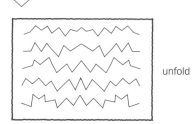

unfold

⬇

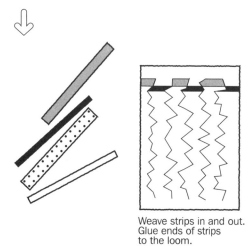

Weave strips in and out.
Glue ends of strips
to the loom.

What shapes can you see in the zigzag pattern?

Investigate how to design a loom for a non-symmetrical weaving like this.

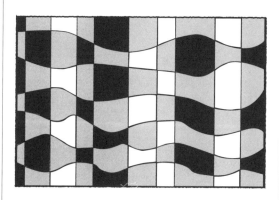

Investigate how to make a weaving with two diamonds like this.

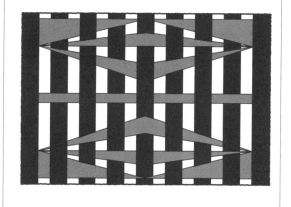

© 1996 Channel Four Learning Ltd **Mathematics from Design** Weaving

3

Decorated container

You need
- ✔ sheets of paper in assorted colours, patterns or textures
- ✔ glue
- ✔ scissors
- ✔ pencil

▶ Choose the materials and method of weaving to design a woven covering for a junk container, such as a cylindrical tube or can.

▶ Measure carefully so that the weaving is the correct height and length to fit the cylinder.

Be safe. If you use a can, ask a parent or your teacher to check it before you start to make sure there are no sharp edges.

▶ Cover several cylinders with woven patterns in the same two colours.

▶ Glue them together to make a decoration or storage pots.

Challenge

You could also try transforming the faces of a junk cuboid into a gift box by covering its faces with a woven pattern.

16 © 1996 Channel Four Learning Ltd **Mathematics from Design** Weaving

4

Woven heart basket

You need

✔ paper in two colours
✔ pencil
✔ ruler
✔ glue
✔ scissors

▶ Cut two rectangles of different-coloured paper 7.5cm wide and 24cm long.

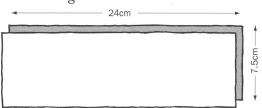

▶ Fold each rectangle in half length-wise.

▶ Round and cut off the corners. (A saucer or small plate will help.)

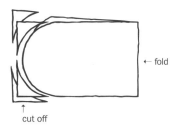

▶ Make two cuts at right angles to the fold to make three strips. See below for measurements. You should have two parts like this, one in each colour.

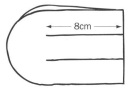

▶ Place one part on top of the other.

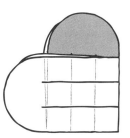

▶ Weave one strip at a time, around and through, carefully.

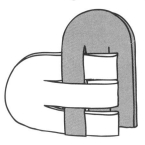

▶ Repeat until all the strips are woven.
Make a handle from scrap paper.

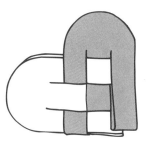

Challenge

Weave a basket in which each strip is a different width.

© 1996 Channel Four Learning Ltd **Mathematics from Design** Weaving

5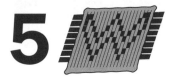

God's Eye weaving

You need

✔ two thin sticks such as garden canes about 15cm long

✔ coloured wools or yarns

✔ small amount of PVA glue

▶ Bind together the two sticks at right angles to each other with a ball of wool.

▶ Tie a knot on top of the binding and cut off the short end of the wool.

▶ Bring the wool over the top of **arm 1** of the cross, wrap the wool all the way around it, ending back where you started. Pull the wool tight.

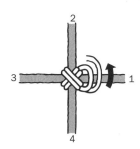

▶ Rotate the sticks a quarter of a turn clockwise. Then bring the wool over the top of **arm 2** and wrap the wool all the way around it.

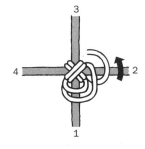

▶ Do the same for **arms 3** and **4**.

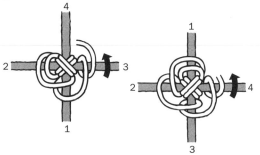

▶ Continue this pattern of weaving. Your **God's Eye** should start to look like this.

▶ To change the colour of wool, tie a double knot in a new colour as close to a stick as possible.

▶ Stop weaving when 1cm of your sticks remain uncovered.

▶ Put a small amount of PVA glue on the arm where you finish and press the wool into it. Then cut off the wool near the stick.

▶ Now think of ways to decorate your God's Eye.

What kinds of symmetry does your God's Eye have?

Challenge

How would you weave a rectangle instead?
Or a kite?
Or a hexagon?

6

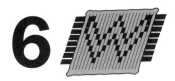

Repeating patterns

The position where the first repeat of weaving **a** starts, is shown by the arrow.

▶ Show where the remaining repeats start on weaving **a**.

▶ Mark where repeats start on weavings **b**, **c** and **d** with arrows.

The code for the first line of weaving **a** is started for you. – **O** means **over** and **U** means **under**. Write the code for the second line.

▶ Then write the codes for weavings **b**, **c** and **d** in the same way, stopping when you get to the first arrow.

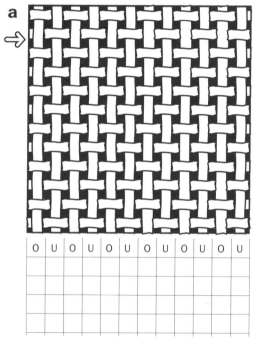

O	U	O	U	O	U	O	U	O	U	O	U

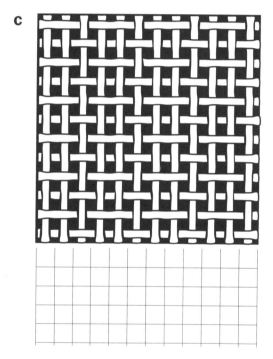

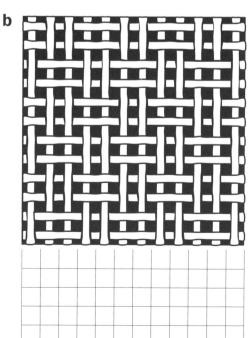

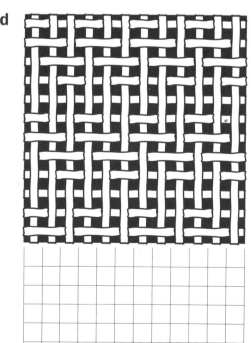

© 1996 Channel Four Learning Ltd **Mathematics from Design** Weaving

Teacher's notes

1
Does it tessellate? page 22

Before starting, ask the children, where have you seen tiling patterns? What makes a tiling pattern different to other patterns? Who needs to use tiles in their work?

In this activity, the children investigate the meaning of 'tessellation' by finding 'tiles' (geometric shapes) which can be fitted together without gaps or overlaps in a systematic and predictable way. (In theory, such patterns should be able to cover an infinite plane.) Some tiles, e.g. rectangular, can be tessellated in different ways and different arrangements compared and discussed.

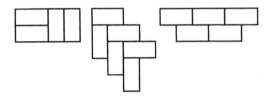

To finish off, the children are asked to generalise their findings on a 2-region Carroll diagram.

☛ Extension: A group investigation. Using 2cm squared grid (adapted from page 44), the children find different ways to tessellate 4cm x 2cm tiles. Some loose tiles cut out in advance to manipulate the tiles before drawing them may help. Three possible solutions are shown in the diagrams above.

2
New tiles from old page 23

This activity uses Pattern Blocks throughout, although each child only needs to be using two at a time. Here the children investigate the effect of taping two matching blocks together along an entire shared edge. They should discover that whatever pair of matching blocks they combine in the way specified, the new shape will always tessellate. Children will enjoy adding detail to the shapes.

They then have to see what happens if two matching shapes are taped together along a partially shared edge.

You may wish to introduce the term 'congruent' to describe shapes which are the same in every detail. The polygonal names for the new shapes can also be discussed e.g. decagon etc.

3
Cut and slide page 24

In this activity, the children learn one technique to transform a rectangle into a unique tessellating unit by dissection and translation.

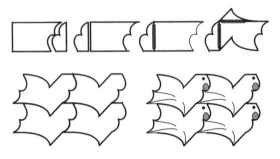

✐ Important questions to raise during or afterwards are:

What is exactly the same about the starting and finishing shape? (They both have the same area.) What about the perimeter? (The perimeter of the new tile will always be longer than that of the rectangle.)

This will clearly show that shapes with the same area do not always have the same perimeter!

Try to find examples of tessellations by Maurits Escher to inspire the children.

☛ Extension: See what happens if you transform a square in the way shown here:

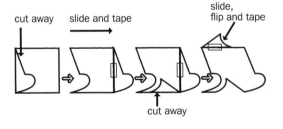

© 1996 Channel Four Learning Ltd **Mathematics from Design** Tiling

4
Tiling pattern *page 25*

In this activity, the children are presented with a square tiling pattern in a particular arrangement and make a different arrangement.

☞ Ask, why do the lines on one tile line up with the lines on other tiles? Measuring will establish that the diagonal stripes are centred on each edge of the tile, a feature commonly found in commercial tiles so that different arrangements can be created.

Tile kits of this type are available for use in school. (See References and resources.)

☞ Variations include:

a A paired or group investigation: Find all possible arrangements made by fitting four of these tiles together in a square formation.

For example:

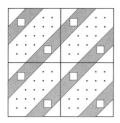 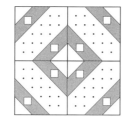

b Design a triangular or hexagonal tile with lines which connect with each other in a similar way.

5
Pentomino tiles *page 26*

In advance, organise the children to work in groups of four, five or six. Make sure they know the meaning of 'congruent' by asking, what can you tell me about congruent shapes?

In this collaborative group activity, the children make eight congruent pentominoes each time and have to try to make these tessellate. (A pentomino is defined on the activity sheet.) For recording the tessellations, 1cm 'broken line' grid is provided on page 46.

After recording the tessellations, the children are challenged to investigate a statement to find out if it is true or false. This involves the children in recognising shapes which are congruent but in different orientations.

The statement is true for there are 12 different pentominoes.

☞ Extension: By making arrangements of five interlocking equilateral triangular tiles and following the same rules, the children investigate the statement "You can also make 12 different shapes using five triangular tiles each time.".

6
Cut and rotate *page 27*

This is a challenging but intriguing activity, requiring perseverance, a systematic approach and accurate measuring and cutting. In it, the children create a tile in which a piece cut from a half-side of a square is rotated 180° about the mid-point. The design is built up in four stages, but at every stage a new tile is created, more complex than the one before.

1st stage   2nd stage

3rd stage   4th stage

The tile will tessellate at each stage. The children can show this by drawing round their new tiles on blank sheets of paper.

This activity may give some insight into how Maurits Escher created some of his inspiring tessellating designs.

☞ Extension: Adapt the basic technique explained on the sheet so that the final tile will have rotational symmetry of order 4.

References and resources

Polydron Tiles (Hope Education)

Clixi Tiles (NES Arnold)

Mathematical Activity Tiles (ATM)

Tiling Diamonds – book and tiles (Shropshire Centre for Mathematics Education)

Problem Solving with Pentominoes (Hope Education)

Pentominoes Jon Millington (Tarquin)

Pattern Blocks (NES Arnold)

The Magic Mirror of Maurits Escher (Tarquin)

Creating Escher-Type Drawings (Jonathan Press)

1 Does it tessellate?

You need
- ✔ templates or stencils of 2-D geometric shapes
- ✔ pencil
- ✔ colouring materials
- ✔ A3 white sheet

▶ This is one way to make squares **tessellate**.

This means you can make them into a tiling pattern without leaving gaps or overlapping them.

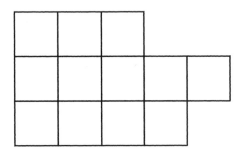

▶ Think of a different way to make squares tessellate.
Draw at least 12 tiles in your pattern.

▶ Choose one shape at a time from the ones below. See if you can make it tessellate.

▶ Choose a tessellation you like. Colour it so that no tiles of the same colour touch along their edges. Use as few colours as possible.

▶ Draw a Carroll diagram like this in your book.
Draw and name shapes in both regions.

These shapes tessellate	These shapes don't tessellate
square	

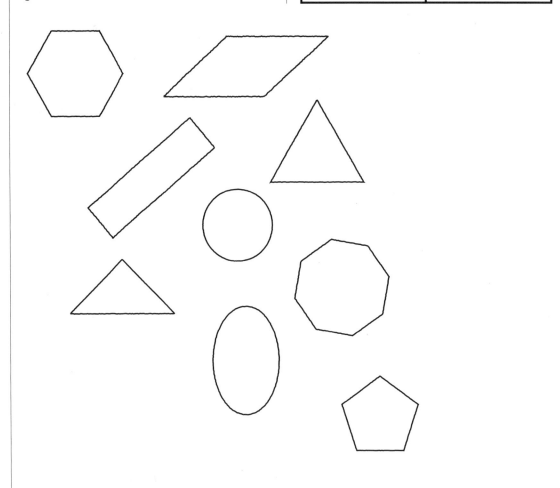

2 New tiles from old

You need
- ✔ Pattern Blocks
- ✔ sticky tape
- ✔ pencil; colouring materials
- ✔ A3 white sheet

▶ Choose two hexagons from a set of Pattern Blocks.
Tape them together along a full edge.

For example:

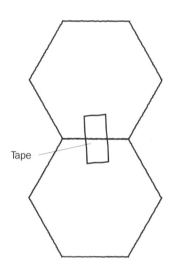

▶ Use the new shape as a tile. Draw it so that it tessellates. Decorate it if you want.

What is the name of the new shape? (Hint: how many sides has it got?)

What would happen if you tried this with other pairs of matching Pattern Blocks?
Can each new shape tessellate? Investigate.

▶ Now try taping a pair of matching Pattern Blocks together so the touching edges do not match (as shown).

For example:

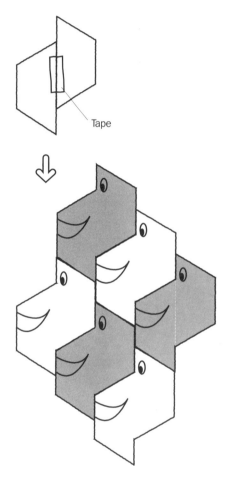

Do pairs of matching blocks taped in this way always tessellate? Investigate.

▶ Write about what you did and what you found.

Challenge

Try to make tiles which will tessellate by taping together three matching blocks along full edges.

© 1996 Channel Four Learning Ltd **Mathematics from Design** Tiling

3 Cut and slide

You need
- ✔ scissors
- ✔ sticky tape
- ✔ rectangles of card about postcard size
- ✔ A3 or A2 white paper
- ✔ colouring materials

▶ Cut, from one edge to a corner of the rectangle, a piece of card like this:

▶ Translate (slide) the cut piece to the opposite side.

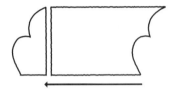

▶ Tape together the two pieces.

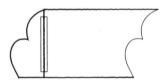

▶ Now do the same for the other two sides.

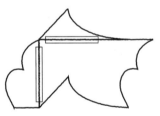

▶ Draw around your shape a number of times.
Try to make it tessellate.

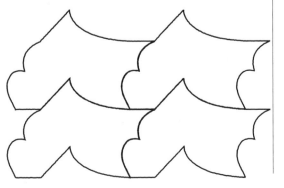

▶ Rotate this slowly.

What does the shape remind you of?

▶ Choose the way up you want it to be. Decorate it if you wish.

How is the rectangle you started with exactly the same as the finished tile?

Challenge

Start with a regular hexagon. Try to make a shape which will tessellate by cutting off and replacing pieces.

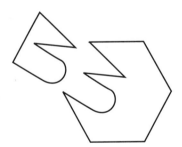

4 Tiling pattern

You need
- ✔ scissors
- ✔ glue
- ✔ A3 or A4 backing sheet

The 25 tiles below show one way of arranging them in a tiling pattern.

▶ Cut out the 25 tiles along the bold lines.

▶ Arrange them in a tiling pattern you like.

▶ Glue your pattern down.

Are there examples of translation, rotation or reflection in your pattern?

How does your arrangement compare with those made by others?

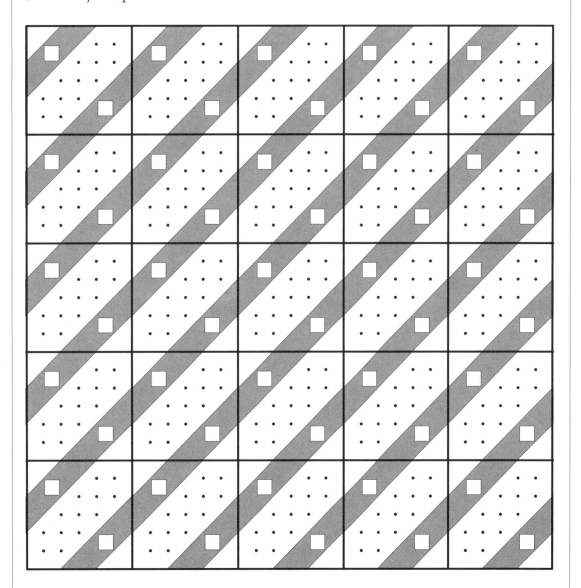

© 1996 Channel Four Learning Ltd **Mathematics from Design** Tiling

5 Pentomino tiles

You need

✔ 40 interlocking square tiles, such as Polydron or Clixi, 10 of each colour

✔ sheet of squared broken-line grid

✔ pencil

✔ colouring materials

Work in a group of four, five or six children for this activity.

1 Agree on a congruent shape you can all make by fitting five tiles together.
Make at least eight of this shape, each shape of one colour.

For example:

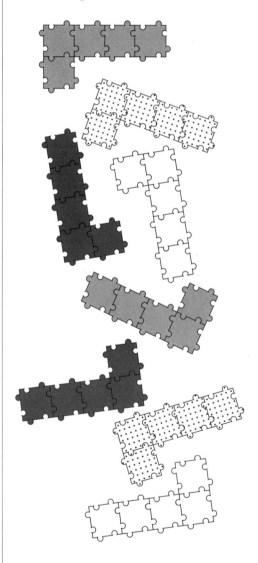

These shapes are called **pentominoes**.

Can you find out why?

2 Tessellate them.

Tessellate means to fit together without gaps or overlaps in a pattern.

You can translate, reflect or rotate the pentominoes as much as you like.

3 Each of you now makes a drawing of the tessellation on a square grid.

4 Repeat **1** to **3**, starting with a different pentomino each time.

True or false? It is possible to make 12 different pentominoes. Investigate.

You are not allowed reflections or rotations of the same pentomino, i.e.

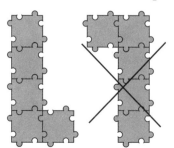 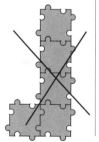

6 Cut and rotate

You need
- ✔ squares of card
- ✔ scissors
- ✔ sticky tape
- ✔ A3 or A2 white paper
- ✔ colouring materials

▶ Mark accurately the mid-point of each side of the card square.

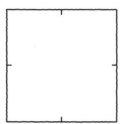

▶ Cut out a piece from half of one side, rotate it about the mid-point. Do not reflect it!

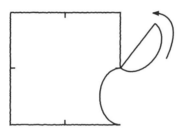

▶ Tape it to the uncut half.

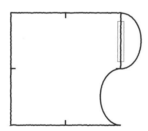

▶ Show that this shape will tessellate.

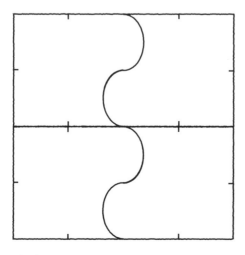

▶ Repeat the 'cut and rotate' process for another side.

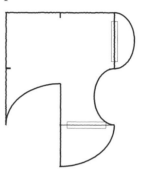

▶ Show that this new shape will tessellate.

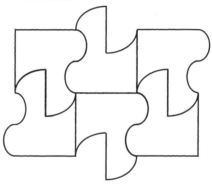

▶ Repeat for a third side and show that this new shape will tessellate.

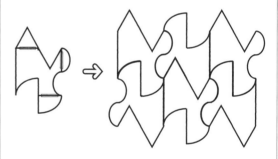

▶ Repeat for a fourth side and show that this new shape will tessellate.

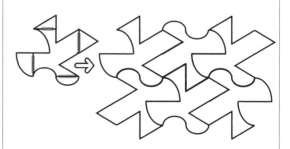

▶ Decorate

© 1996 Channel Four Learning Ltd **Mathematics from Design** Tiling

Folding

Teacher's notes

1
Spring things *page 30*

Instructions for making a paper 'concertina' spring are given on this activity sheet. To make this the children have to use and interpret mathematical vocabulary and fold systematically. Sometimes, this construction is called 'Jacob's Ladder'.

The repetitive movement needed for successful construction of the spring is applied mathematics. Patterns can take many different forms, e.g. shape, colour, texture, size, orientation and repetitive movements such as those in Maypole dancing.

Once the basic construction is mastered, the children are encouraged to design an object on which the springs can feature. To encourage perseverance and creativity, you could organise a class competition for the most original design.

☞ Springs are mathematical constructions, with close links with technology. Can the children bring in examples of springs or make a list of where springs are used? Why are they useful and needed? What kind of paper makes the 'springiest' paper springs? What fair test could be designed to investigate?

2
Double star *page 31*

This is a collaborative group activity. Before undertaking it, make sure children know what an isosceles triangle is. Also ask, how are the A4 (larger) and A5 sheets the same? Different? The children should note that two A5 sheets are equivalent to one A4 sheet.

Although A4 and A5 paper is suggested for the construction by paper-folding of isosceles triangles, the instructions work for any papers in the A series since each A-size rectangular sheet is made by folding in half the size numerically below it. As a result, a series of similar rectangles is produced, i.e. the sides of any A-size paper are in the ratio $1:\sqrt{2}$ or $1: 1.4142...$

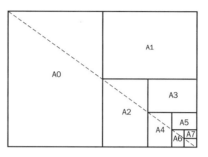

☛ Extension: The children make A6 and A7 paper by careful folding and cutting. They experiment with overlaying several different sizes of isosceles triangles and investigate the effect of putting several of the triangles together.

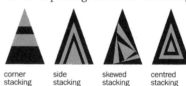

corner stacking · side stacking · skewed stacking · centred stacking

Links with tiling and symmetry can be discussed.

3
Imagining *page 32*

It is important that children are given opportunities to visualise shapes, including 2-D representations of 3-D objects. Some children are particularly adept at this. For this activity, the children have to fold 'in their heads' shapes made from five interlocking square tiles and decide which of these will fold to make open cubes. Of the 12 possible arrangements of five square tiles (often called pentominoes), these eight are nets for open cubes:

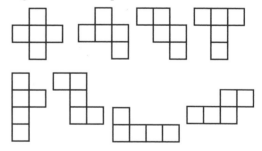

If six tiles are joined together in the same way (hexominoes), as suggested in the **Challenge** 11 of the 35 possible arrangements are nets for cubes.

☛ Extension: Choose the materials and the mathematics to make a card copy with the same dimensions as the cube (open or closed) made from the interlocking tiles.

© 1996 Channel Four Learning Ltd **Mathematics from Design** Folding

4
Tissue tiles *page 33*

In this activity, the children transform tissue-paper circles into squares by paper-folding and discover how the shapes created by the overlaps can be used to enhance a tiling pattern. Before the sheet is given out, provide paper circles and ask the children to try and transform a circle into a square by paper folding only – no measuring or cutting is allowed, then compare results.

If available, the tissue shapes can be held in position against a window with an OHP transparency – its static properties hold the shapes in place. Otherwise, shapes glued lightly to tracing paper can be displayed similarly.

☛ Extensions include:
a finding other shapes that the children can construct accurately from tissue circles;
b experimenting with folding randomly or systematically large sheets of tissue paper to create shapes in the overlaps.

5
Magic grid *page 34*

This activity provides opportunities for revising vocabulary relating to circles and for recognising a range of geometric shapes. By following instructions, the children will end up with an isometric grid like this:

Encourage the children to look for, describe or name shapes made by combining two or more equilateral triangles. These include:

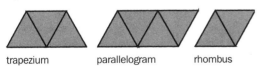

trapezium   parallelogram   rhombus

💬 Discussion can also focus on similar shapes, e.g. how many different sizes of equilateral triangles can be seen? Are there any similar rhombi? etc.

☛ Extension activities include:

a extending the 'family' of equilateral triangles until a predictable growth pattern can be spotted, i.e. the sequence of square numbers;

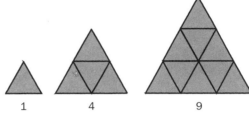

1   4   9

b working out how many equilateral triangles are on the grid. (The answer is not 24!)

6
Fold and cut back 1 *page 35*

This activity requires a systematic approach and the ability to concentrate but since the resultant design is so aesthetically pleasing, most children will show these qualities. Triangles are successively cut and folded back using given rules to create a pattern which has some symmetrical and some asymmetrical elements, a feature which can be usefully discussed.

💬 Ask, what is the relationship between the starting square and the final design? This is to see if the children realise that the black paper covers an area of 100cm^2 regardless of how far it has 'spread' over the paper.

☛ Extensions:
Once the basic technique is mastered, the children can experiment freely or be given more complicated rules to follow, e.g. to create a design in which:

a all lines are perpendicular to each other;
b each cut-out shape is a pentagon (or other nominated polygon);
c the overall result has one line of symmetry.

References and resources

Paper Magic: Folding Polygons, William Gibbs and Liz Meenan, (Educational Television Company) c/o Tarquin

Tissue Paper Circles (Philip & Tacey)

Folds – Leapfrog Action Book (Tarquin)

Spring things

You need

✔ glue

✔ long strips of paper in at least two colours, 2cm to 3cm wide

1 Take two strips of paper of different colours and glue the ends at right angles to each other.

2 Fold the horizontal strip to the right.

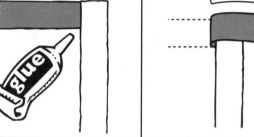

3 Fold the vertical strip upwards.

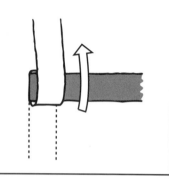

4 Fold the horizontal strip to the left.

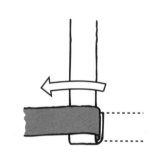

5 Fold the vertical strip downwards.

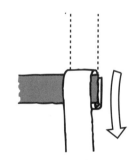

6 Repeat the last four steps until the strips are used up. Then glue the ends.

▶ Try to think of something interesting to make with the paper springs.

Challenge

What would happen if you used two strips of paper ...

each a different length?
each a different width?
each a different kind of paper?

© 1996 Channel Four Learning Ltd **Mathematics from Design** Folding

Double star

You need
- ✔ sheets of A4 and A5 paper in two colours
- ✔ scrap A4 paper
- ✔ large backing sheet

▶ Work in a group of three or four children to do this.

▶ Practise paper-folding **isosceles triangles** on scrap A4 paper. Like this:

Fold edge to edge.

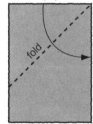 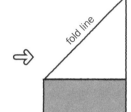

Fold edge to edge.

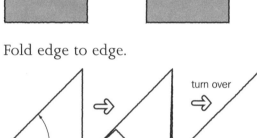

▶ Now make two isoceles triangles using different-coloured A4 paper and A5 paper.

▶ Centre the smaller triangle on top of the larger one.

▶ Plan together how to make an eight-pointed star like this.

© 1996 Channel Four Learning Ltd **Mathematics from Design** Folding

3

Imagining

You need
✔ Five interlocking square tiles such as Polydron or Clixi

▶ Make an **open cube** with the **five tiles**.
Don't unfold it until you are told to later on.
Don't use any other tiles to help.

Some of 12 shapes below can be folded to make open cubes.

▶ Imagine folding each shape in your head.
Put ✔ in the circle if you think it will make an open cube.

▶ Afterwards, break up your open cube and use the tiles to check your results.

Put ✔ in the triangle if the shape folds to make an open cube.

Challenge

Each shape which makes a cube is called a **net**.
Get an extra tile and make **a closed cube**.
Draw shapes you think will make nets for this.
Check your results.

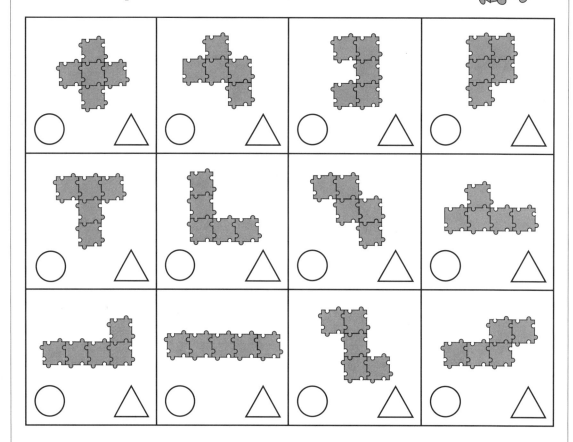

© 1996 Channel Four Learning Ltd **Mathematics from Design** Folding

Tissue tiles

You need
- ✔ tissue-paper circles in at least two colours
- ✔ backing sheet of tracing or greaseproof paper
- ✔ glue

▶ Imagine: Before you read on, how could you transform a circle into an accurate square?

One way is to:

▶ Fold a tissue circle into quarters as shown.
▶ Crease the folds well.

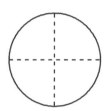

▶ Now carefully make these folds to transform the circle into a square. Using a ruler may help.
▶ Crease the folds well.

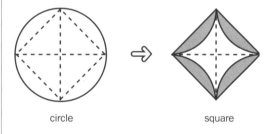

circle   square

▶ Make three other squares in the same way, two in each colour.

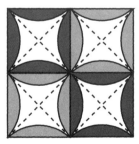

▶ Flip the squares over.

▶ Position your squares on a backing sheet of tracing paper. Put tiny dots of glue at each corner to attach them.

Add more squares if you want.

How could you make regular octagons by paper-folding? Would they tessellate?

Challenge

With some friends, and the help of shape stencils, try to plan a star like this by paper-folding circles.

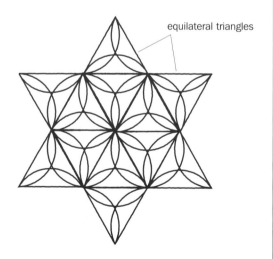

equilateral triangles

© 1996 Channel Four Learning Ltd **Mathematics from Design** Folding

Magic grid

You need
- ✔ A4 paper
- ✔ pair of compasses
- ✔ ruler
- ✔ colouring materials
- ✔ pencil

▶ Construct a circle with radius 6cm.

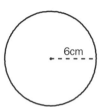

▶ Mark off the 6cm radius on the circumference six times.

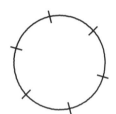

▶ Join up the six points on the circumference to form a regular hexagon.
▶ Cut out the hexagon accurately.

▶ Fold along three lines of symmetry to get six equilateral triangles.
▶ Crease the folds well.

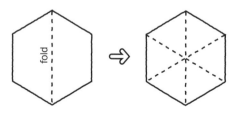

▶ Take one edge and fold as shown.
▶ Crease well and unfold.

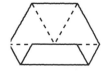

▶ Repeat for the other five edges. Your design should now look like this:

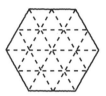

Can you see a rhombus, a parallelogram, a trapezium and a smaller regular hexagon? What other shapes can you see?

▶ Now plan how to colour your grid.

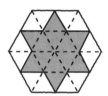

One way is to draw a six-pointed star.

▶ Make other grids in the same way.
Plan different patterns to draw on each one.

Challenge

Find out how to construct a regular octagon.

What happens if you fold it in the same way?

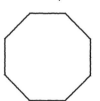

© 1996 Channel Four Learning Ltd **Mathematics from Design** Folding

6

Cut and fold back 1

You need
- ✔ scissors
- ✔ glue
- ✔ 10cm x 10cm square of black paper
- ✔ A3 white backing sheet

▶ Don't apply any glue until your pattern is complete.

1 Cut a triangle from one side of the square.
Reflect the triangle and position as shown.

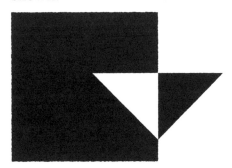

2 Cut a second triangle from the black triangle.
Reflect the smaller triangle and position as shown.

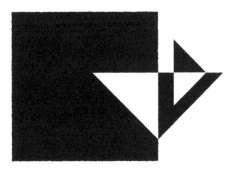

3 Cut a triangle from another side of the square.
Reflect it and position as shown.

4 Repeat step **2** for the second black triangle.

5 Repeat steps **1** to **4** for the other two sides.

6 Cut out extra triangles if you want, but you must cut and reflect them in the same way.

7 Glue the pieces, starting from the centre.

Plan the cuts and folds so that the design has rotational symmetry of order 4.

© 1996 Channel Four Learning Ltd **Mathematics from Design** Folding

Reflecting

Teacher's notes

1
How many ways? *page 38*

Here the children find different ways of arranging up to four geometric-plane shapes so that each combination has a line of symmetry. Encourage the children to draw their solutions in different orientations, horizontally, vertically and diagonally. You may wish to introduce the term 'bilateral' (having two sides) symmetry to describe such shapes. Logic blocks with hexagons and related stencils can be used for this. It is a good estimating task since the children need to position the shapes by 'trial and improve' to make them balance. Encourage the use of mirrors for checking the accuracy of the lines of symmetry. Can the children name or learn polygonal names for any of the combined shapes?

If each child contributes one or two designs, each on a small card, these can be sorted in different ways using criteria suggested by you or the children. To make the display interactive, children can also add further examples to the sets whilst on display.

☛ Extension: How many different ways can the children join all four given shapes so that each way has one line of symmetry?

2
Cut and fold back 2 *page 39*

This activity sheet gives instructions for creating a pattern by following simple rules. The children are then asked to consider in what way their design is symmetrical and not symmetrical. (It will have symmetry of shape but not of colour.) This can lead to discussion of positive and negative shapes.

symmetry of shape   symmetry of shape but not colour

Afterwards, the choice of challenges requires the children to use and apply their knowledge of symmetry and of skills introduced in the basic activity.

☛ Extension: The children fold a square of paper in four quarters, cut pieces from all four layers simultaneously and arrange the pieces systematically to make a design with rotational symmetry of order 4.

3
Model symmetry *page 40*

The children investigate the effect of using the same starter shape to create different arrangements with two lines of symmetry. Only four arrangements are possible if the tiles are fitted together to make one shape.

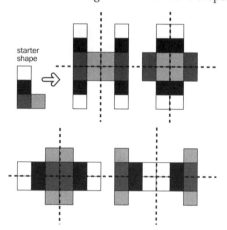

After using the given starter shape, the children can make their own and create patterns in the same way. The children should be able to generalise that there are only four possible arrangements, using the 'rules' given.

If interlocking tiles are in short supply, congruent paper squares in at least four colours can be used instead and the individual squares of the starter shape taped together.

☛ Extensions include:

a Four equilateral triangular tiles can be used as the starter tiles along with an isometric grid. What patterns can be created if one side is a line of symmetry and the shape is 'flipped' repeatedly?

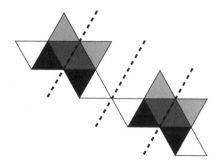

© 1996 Channel Four Learning Ltd **Mathematics from Design** Reflecting

b A paired or small-group activity: Using a 'starter tile' (made with four squares) as shown on the activity sheet, how many different patterns with two lines of symmetry can be created on a 6x6 grid marked like this? One solution is shown on the grid.

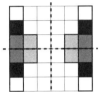

4
Picture gallery *page 41*

In advance, get the children to work in pairs and to study each other's faces. Which features on the partner's face are symmetrical? Are they perfectly symmetrical? What about jewellery? What about symmetry in nature?

The follow-up activity provides the opportunity for children to build up a symmetrical design based on the theme of faces. Make available as many different types of paper and card as you can, including scrap pieces and simple collage materials. As far as possible, let the children develop their own strategies for the creation and positioning of the symmetrical parts. Encourage the children to make some 3-D features to add interest. The hair may only be approximately symmetrical but this is the case in real life!

☛ Extensions include:

a Children making an observational line drawing of a friend's face (or their own if a mirror is available);
b Cutting vertically into two symmetrical halves a colour photograph of a face from a magazine. Each child takes one half and tries to draw the missing half. How do the results compare?

5
Find the mirror line *page 42*

Using a mirror the children have to find where to position it to make a given set of shapes from one starter shape. All of the 'new' shapes have one line of symmetry, either horizontal, diagonal or vertical. One possible set of solutions is:

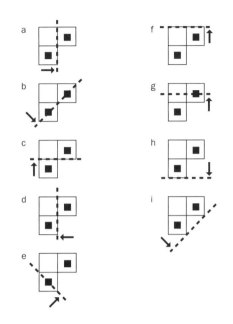

mirror line - - - - - - -
direction of the mirror →

☛ Extension: The children can hinge together two mirrors, position them at right angles to each other on the starter shape, then draw shapes found and the mirror lines.

6
Paper cut-outs *page 43*

The children cut symmetrical shapes with given properties from squares of paper. The children will need to observe detail carefully, visualise, work systematically and use 'trial and improve' methods. They can prepare their own squares of paper by cutting and folding A4 or A5 paper.

This diagonal fold is one of those needed to solve the problems in the most efficient way, since all of the four shapes illustrated need to be cut from squares folded in this way:

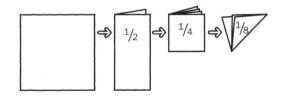

References and resources

Fun Figures, Michael Grater (Macdonald)

Safety Mirrors, Taskmaster

The Mirror Puzzle Book, Marion Walter (Tarquin)

Maths in Colour, Wendy and David Clemson (Stanley Thornes Ltd)

© 1996 Channel Four Learning Ltd **Mathematics from Design** Reflecting

1R

How many ways?

You need
- stencils or templates of geometric shapes
- mirror for checking
- unlined paper

▶ Make new shapes with the ones shown, using the rules shown below each time:

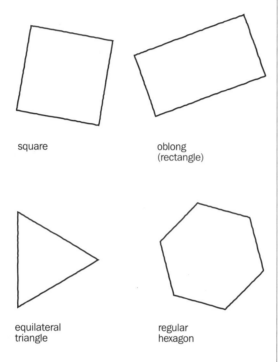

square

oblong (rectangle)

equilateral triangle

regular hexagon

Rules:
- Use at least two different shapes each time.
- Draw shapes so that they touch each other.
- The new shape should have one line of symmetry.
- Draw the line of symmetry.

For example:

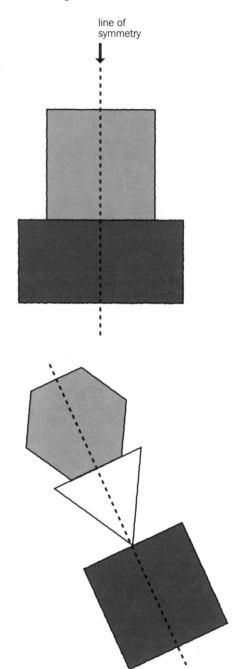

How many different shapes can you find?

Choose four shapes of your own, some with curved sides.

Make more symmetrical shapes.

© 1996 Channel Four Learning Ltd **Mathematics from Design** Reflecting

2R

Cut and fold back 2

You need

✔ A4 and A3 sheets of paper in contrasting colours

✔ glue

✔ scissors

▶ Cut several different shapes out of one longer side of the A4 sheet. Lay them in order as you cut them out.

▶ Glue the rest of the sheet onto an A3 sheet as shown:

▶ Now flip (reflect) the shapes you cut out and make a pattern like this. Don't glue yet.

▶ Glue when you have checked carefully.

In what way is your pattern symmetrical?
In what way is it not symmetrical?

Now plan how to make a pattern like one of these:

© 1996 Channel Four Learning Ltd **Mathematics from Design** Reflecting

3R

Model symmetry

You need

✔ 16 interlocking square tiles such as Polydron or Clixi, 4 each of 4 colours

✔ 1cm squared grid

You need 16 interlocking square tiles such as Polydron or Clixi, four each of four colours; 1cm squared grid; colouring pencils.

Key

▶ Make this starter shape

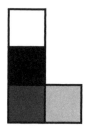

▶ Now add the other 12 tiles to make this model with two lines of symmetry.

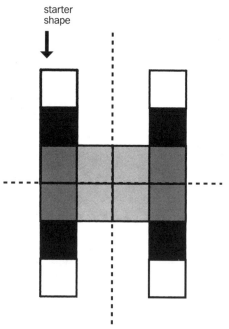

▶ Record your model on the 1cm squared grid. Show lines of symmetry.

▶ Now use this starter shape and add the other 12 tiles to complete a new model with two lines of symmetry. Record the model.

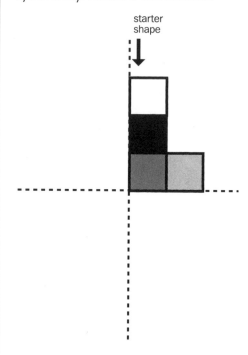

▶ Find two other ways to use the starter shape to create a model with two lines of symmetry. Record the models you find on 1cm squared grid.

▶ Compare your models with a friend's.

Make a starter shape with at least five tiles.

Make and record models with two lines of symmetry in the same way.

40

© 1996 Channel Four Learning Ltd **Mathematics from Design** Reflecting

Picture gallery

▶ Cut a symmetrical face shape about the same size as your face from card.

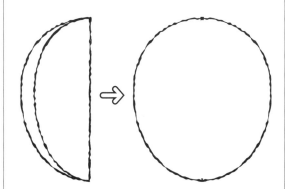

▶ Glue on symmetrical features made from paper or card e.g. eyes, mouth, ears, nose, beard, spectacles, jewellery, hair, etc. Make the features balance about the line of symmetry.

▶ You can make curly hair by 'stretching' strips of paper with a pair of blunt scissors or blunt knife.

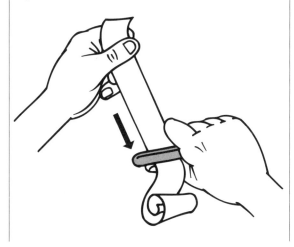

Or wind a strip in a spiral around a pencil and slide off.

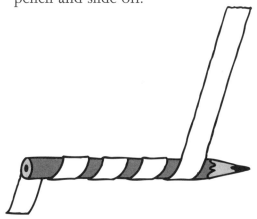

If you make curly hair, glue it on to be as symmetrical as you can.

Perhaps your teacher will display the faces – if they're not too frightening!

▶ Look at your face in a mirror.

Does everything you see have line symmetry?

You need
- ✔ Assorted papers and cards (assorted colours)
- ✔ glue
- ✔ scissors

© 1996 Channel Four Learning Ltd **Mathematics from Design** Reflecting

Find the mirror line

You need
- ✔ a small mirror
- ✔ pencil
- ✔ ruler

▶ Try to make all the shapes below starting with this shape each time.

▶ Draw the mirror line and the way the mirror is facing each time using an arrow.
The first one is done for you.

Challenge

Draw any new shapes you can make using the starter shape.

Show the mirror line and the way the mirror is facing.

a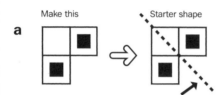

b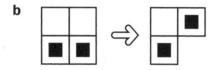

c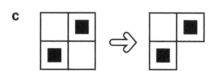

d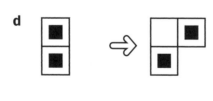

e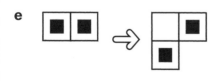

f

g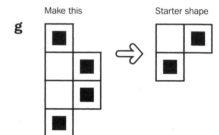

h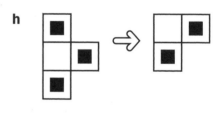

i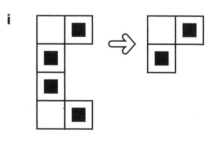

j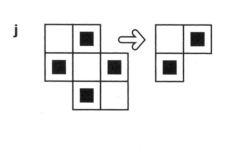

© 1996 Channel Four Learning Ltd **Mathematics from Design** Reflecting

6R

Paper cut-outs

You need

✔ Squares (at least 10cm x 10cm) of scrap and 'best' paper
✔ scissors
✔ ruler
✔ pencil
✔ paper
✔ glue

▶ Here are four symmetrical shapes made by folding then cutting squares of paper.

▶ Try to make enlarged copies of them by folding and cutting paper.

▶ Do trial versions on scrap paper first.

▶ In your book, glue down in order the trial versions, then your 'best' version of one shape. Write about what you did.

What is the same about these four shapes?

Challenge

Now try to make a cut-out version of this.

© 1996 Channel Four Learning Ltd **Mathematics from Design** Reflecting

Squared dotty grid (1cm)

Isometric grid (1cm)

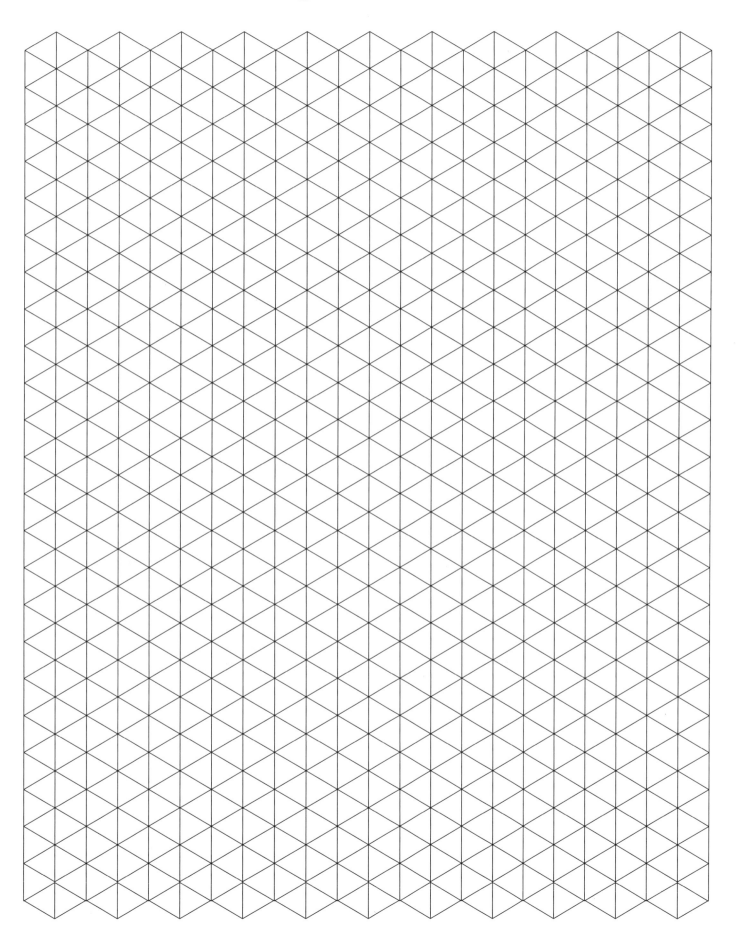

Squared broken-line grid (1cm)

Name of child
_____

Mathematics from Design
Activity-page record sheet

Activities completed **Extension** **Additional comments**

Printing
1 Printing puzzle
2 Monoprint
3 Carbon-paper printing
4 Overlaps
5 Four-square patterns
6 Alphabet prints

Weaving
1 Paper looms
2 Symmetrical paper looms
3 Decorated container
4 Woven heart basket
5 God's Eye weaving
6 Repeating patterns

Tiling
1 Does it tessellate?
2 New tiles from old
3 Cut and slide
4 Tiling pattern
5 Pentomino tiles
6 Cut and rotate

Folding
1 Spring things
2 Double star
3 Imagining
4 Tissue tiles
5 Magic grid
6 Cut and fold back 1

Reflecting
1 How many ways?
2 Cut and fold back 2
3 Model symmetry
4 Picture gallery
5 Find the mirror line
6 Paper cut-outs

© 1996 Channel Four Learning Ltd **Mathematics from Design**

Additional information

Useful addresses
Send for catalogues from the following for a wide range of suitable materials:
▶ Association of Teachers of Mathematics, 7 Shaftesbury Street, Derby DE23 8YB
▶ Tarquin Publications, Stradbroke, Diss, Norfolk IP21 5JP
▶ The Mathematical Association, 259 London Road, Leicester LE2 3BE
▶ Jonathan Press/Claire Publications, Unit 8, Tey Brook Craft Centre, Great Tey, Colchester, Essex CO6 1JE
▶ Pictorial Charts Education Trust (PCET), 257 Kirchen Road, London W13 0UD

Magazines
Art and Craft in Education (monthly), Scholastic Publications, Villiers House, Clarendon Avenue, Leamington Spa CV32 5PR
The Big Paper: Exploring Primary Art, Design and Technology (termly), Gillian Welsh, Chester Court, High Street, Knowle, Solihull B93 0LL

Children's books
The Amazing Book of Shapes, Lydia Sharman (Dorling Kindersley Ltd, 9 Henrietta Street, London WC2E 8PS)

Teacher's books
Mathematics through Art and Design, Anne Woodman & Eric Albany (Collins Educational, 77–85 Fulham Palace Road, Hammersmith, London W6 8JB)
Maths in Colour, Wendy & David Clemson (Stanley Thornes)
Simply Artistic, Joan Chambers & Molly Hood (Belair Publications Ltd, PO Box 12, Twickenham TW1 2QL)
Material Pleasures, Lilian Coppock (Belair Publications Ltd)

Software
Video Maths Computer Software, GSN Educational Software Ltd, 50 Stamford Street, Ashton-under-Lyne, Lancashire OL6 6QH